A Radical Solution for the Problems of
Bankruptcy and Financial Bottlenecks
for Individuals and Companies

A Radical Solution for the Problems of Bankruptcy and Financial Bottlenecks for Individuals and Companies

Mohammed Hassan Alzahrani

Translated by
Ali Cherni

To order additional copies of this book, contact:
Xlibris Corporation
0-800-644-6988
www.xlibrispublishing.co.uk
Orders@xlibrispublishing.co.uk
304406

Contents

Dedicated to all the people in the world who suffer from financial problems and in pursuit of the most suitable solutions

Poverty is one of the major reasons for all the unending demonstrations and uprisings people mount against their governments all around the world. The staggering spread of such phenomenon has led to significant psychological pressures befalling innumerable communities, whose natural reaction would involve waging demonstration after demonstration in the hope that their living conditions might soon change. Some of the demonstrations may lose its non-violent tag and turn into riots, causing chaos in the streets and public squares. This, in turn, can have damaging consequences with the loss of human life and property, as well as endangering other people's lives for the sake of achieving better living standards. Unsurprisingly, in most rich countries, there are hardly any social-driven demonstrations that result in such alarming anarchy and threat to human life. One can safely argue that poverty is the main reason behind all these demonstrations, particularly in developing countries.

> **Upon request, the contents of the program can be disclosed to the relevant investing government agencies.**
>
> *www.quland.org*

This project contains the following topics:

Individuals

Silver Package: Advantages, requirements and method of use, and conditions

Gold Package: Advantages, requirements and method of use, and conditions

Companies

Silver Package: Advantages, requirements and method of use, and conditions

Gold Package: Advantages, requirements and method of use, and conditions

In the Name of God, Most Gracious, Most Merciful

Introduction

First of all, all praise be to God alone and prayers and peace upon our Prophet Muhammad and his family.

Over the last few years, the global economy has seen a dramatic downturn due to the credit crunch. There have also been alarming signs of an imminent collapse in the financial markets, with instability and economic uncertainty becoming all the more the characterising aspect of the business world. As a result, these conditions have had a negative impact on the economic activities of the different companies, including major corporations being potentially exposed to bankruptcy and going under. Therefore, as a personal endeavour, this book aims to provide some appropriate solutions regarding the right of the company to remain strong in the market, the right of the employee to maintain his position, and to reduce the size of unemployment in the community as the bankruptcy of these multinational companies adds significantly to the spread of unemployment. It is, thus, possible to develop alternative solutions to reduce the bankruptcy of companies and institutions. As such, this programme seeks to support these companies and institutions, using an interest-free policy in return for liquidity and a commitment to reduce the size of unemployment. By developing a specific programme, the author intends to reduce the size of unemployment and the bankruptcy of financially insolvent companies, in addition to providing liquidity for several companies and institutions.

This programme is considered one of the most important programmes to be provided by the author who has been preparing it since 25 February 1432 AH (29 January 2011). The programme aims to improve the economic structure as it provides liquidity for those interested in investing their money but feel insecure in terms of how to appropriately do so, given the precarious economic situation. Thus, this programme allows for the provision of interest-free loans, provided that a certain fund is deposited for the authority, which determines an interest-free option and allows people, through the programme, the chance to attain lucrative repayment benefits. This programme also introduces the idea of buying shares for investment purposes to all customers, including individuals and companies, while providing liquidity and reducing the financial bottlenecks. It also attempts to eliminate, or at least minimise, the problem of unemployment and poverty in the Arab and Western societies.

How Does a Personal Account Work?

It deals with opening a personal account to provide liquidity and to work out ratios of the incoming funds as there are many people who are well-off but still suffer from financial problems, with their salaries hardly covering their needs till the end of the month. As such, the present publication offers a convenient method to collect money by means of opening a personal account for all working people who have a desire to provide liquidity at times of need and allocate a certain percentage of the incoming funds to be added to the sums that are collected on a weekly basis.

We will next examine the following in more detail:

1. An idea about the programme for individuals and companies.
2. The problems of poverty in the world.
3. Unemployment rates and its impact on society.
4. Companies, institutions, and the factors contributing to their bankruptcy.
5. The role of companies and institutions in the reduction of unemployment.
6. How does a personal account work?
7. The most effective solutions to combat poverty, unemployment, as well as corporate bankruptcies and ways to reduce them.

About the Programme

Several researchers and economic analysts have attempted to find solutions to the issues of unemployment and poverty, which can disastrously result in the spread of corruption and crimes within the most affected communities, where these problems are usually rife. There appears to be some solutions for the elimination of unemployment or at least minimising it, with several researchers providing a number of solutions to this problem. Some of the main solutions include the achievement of the principle of equality and social justice, the provision of interest-free loans for graduates, or offering monthly subsidies for the unemployed. However, the deliberate intention of governments in some countries to disregard these solutions may have caused the state to lose so much money.

Therefore, this programme has been designed, namely, the Radical Solutions to the Problems of Bankruptcy and Financial Bottlenecks for Individuals and Companies, which will be submitted to government agencies or banks wishing to endorse it. *The most important advantages of this programme include as follows:*

1. This programme targets all segments of society – the unemployed, the lowly paid, the minimum-wage and minimum-income holders, government employees, private sector employees, and also all small businesses and large firms.

2. To minimise poverty and unemployment and to reduce the negative effects resulting from the actions of people suffering from these issues, such as falling into crime.

3. This programme is designed in a manner to ensure that the responsible body take the necessary guarantees, enabling customers to take advantage of the programme.

4. To reduce the bankruptcy of companies, as this causes increased unemployment rates.

This programme was originally started on 25 February 1432 (AH), corresponding to 29 January 2011 (AD). Initially, the idea behind this programme involved reducing the phenomenon of corporate bankruptcies; then, it developed to include government officials and private sector employees, as well as a large segment of society not covered by the benefits of this programme, such as the unemployed and the poor classes. The situation of the latter had been particularly monitored in this study for a certain period of time until a programme was finally designed for this category, whose presence in the community has recently become too apparent because of the financial crisis engulfing everyone. As the programme has been developed for all classes in the society, the details of this programme will be provided to interested parties wishing to endorse and implement it according to Islamic laws so that customers can take advantage of this programme and achieve the desired outcomes and appropriate solutions for any financial predicaments. *Some of the most important goals of this programme include the following: Material gains*, through which the customer can take advantage of the packages provided and to obtain financing in proportion to the package chosen. The programme-implementing agency may also take advantage of the amounts deposited by the customers and use them for investment purposes. *Security objective:* It is widely agreed that there are people languishing under the burden of poverty and unemployment, which can lead to psychological pressure and push them to extreme and abnormal behaviours. As a result, a large number of crimes, such as fraud, swindling, theft, and murder, start to hit society. Thus, this programme aims to reduce unemployment and poverty and to minimise their negative impacts. *Political objective:* What is happening in the world in terms of people's demonstrations against their governments can be ascribed to the most important causes, namely, poverty and unemployment. As such, this programme is designed to include the largest section of society and to eliminate all these unfortunate events.

Individuals

Many people resort to bank loans to meet their basic needs; however, they may find these loans too difficult to repay even when the bank had provided finance for the client. Still, a large number of the beneficiaries may be forced to re-finance again from the bank before settling the first loan, which causes them all sorts of problems. In most of these instances, interest rates can vary from one bank to another, and they often range between 3.80% and 4.50%. Despite the offers given by some banks, the interest rates can still represent a major dilemma for some people. However, since only these offers are available, many people feel obliged to accept them because of their need for funds.

We often become extremely worried due to the insufficiency of our monthly salaries, and many of us frequently suffer recurrent financial crises. Strange enough is the fact that many who earn high monthly salaries may still be unable to cover their end-of-the-month expenses. The question that begs to be answered is then whether this is due to the weakness of financial resources or the mishandling of the incoming amounts.

Table 1: Distribution of individuals according to their standards of living

Available Amount (SAR)	Interest Rates (%)	Expenses	Income (SAR)	Class
150–350	10	Bills + clothing + food	1,500–3,500	Poor classes
1,000–3,750	25	Bills + clothing + food	4,000–15,000	Low incomers
5,600–14,000	35	Bills + clothing + food	16,000–40,000	Upper classes

Table 1 shows percentage of net rates for each class according to income and circumstances.

Dividing People According to Their Dealings with Public Events

In any community, there are countless events and celebrations, which can be extremely costly and sometimes beyond the financial capabilities of a number of people who may find themselves unable to cope in the face of rising prices and the high cost of dowries and marriage-ceremony venues and furniture. As a result, those seeking to get married often miss on the right opportunity to collect as much money as possible as there are three social categories, with each category having its own way in dealing with these events:

- **Category One:** It includes those who do not worry about the costs associated with marriage, that is, the wealthy. These are not normally interested in the timing of their wedding, whether in the short or the long run, because they have sufficient resources. Thus, money is not of an issue in their case.
- **Category Two:** Included in this category are most people who will have to tie the knot on their partners and decide on whether they can get married based on their financial situation in order to be able to collect as much money as possible to cover all the relevant costs. Often, deciding on this can take one year or more.
- **Category Three:** This involves the poor, especially if the husband is poor and the people of his wife are self-sufficient.

These people are not often in regular employment, and even if they are employed, they are not well-paid. Thus, they cannot obtain a loan from the bank because of the low monthly income. In some cases, these low incomers may get married after a long period; while in other instances, the relationship may end in separation due to either the intolerance of the wife's family to the husband's poverty or to his financial inability to support and meet his wife's expenses, including accommodation and other related costs. Again, money is at the heart of it all. Added to this are the increasingly high prices of food and consumables, which largely affects some categories with low income and those from poorer classes.

Along with the increasing showers expensive prices of foodstuffs and consumer items, impacting seriously on some groups experiencing limited income and poor class.

If we look at the food, we find a marked increase in prices, and another look at consumables, we find the same problem and then to the world of real estate to find the height increases. What are the reasons that led to high prices? There are several points that have been identified the real reasons for the higher prices.

There are several factors – monopolisation and exploitation of some traders and not to fear God and forget about controlling them, greed and inflation, and also the high prices of basic components. Sometimes many people, wishing to invest funds securely and comfortably at the same time, quickly spend this money refunded without interest to the money either cashed in life or in stock trading or in some projects doomed to fail sometimes.

Next, some global poverty issues will be reviewed. In addition, unemployment and its impact on individuals and society alike will be discussed, while the factors leading to corporate bankruptcy and the role of companies in terms of reducing the widespread unemployment, as well as developing the appropriate solutions for these problems will be approached.

Problems of Poverty in the World

The concept of poverty points to a particular class in society suffering from rejection and deprivation of all basic requirements of a decent living. Thus, poverty is an economic state, whereby an individual finds it very difficult to gain sufficient funds, allowing him or her to obtain adequate housing or purchase a much needed means of transport, along with all other indispensable life necessities.

On a global note, poverty is divided into five levels distributed across the members of the community, and they are as follows:

Underclass: At the bottom of the social hierarchy, this is a social class where people do not have the adequate means to provide for education due to absence of sufficient income, if at all, and proper housing. In most cases, these people are found in run-down houses or huts that do not protect them from the natural elements such as the freezing winter cold. Often, people in this category do not have a regular monthly income, as they live on seasonal or petty jobs.

Special needs: This is a class of people who have disabilities preventing them from regular movement and from properly conducting day-to-day activities. They often have a monthly income paid to them by the social services but may not be sufficient to meet all their life needs.

Low-certificate holders: This includes a certain type of people whose own personal circumstances prevented them from pursuing their education. They often have a job with a very basic monthly income; otherwise, they could be still looking for a suitable job to meet their basic needs and might not be able to obtain whatever they want due to the lack of the appropriate competencies required by the government agencies or the private sector.

University graduates: This involves those who have certificates but are still hunting for a job suited to their qualifications due to the lack of vacancies. For example, the percentage of job seekers in the Arab world reached 18% of the total population.

Divorced women and widows: This class constitutes a large proportion in the community because of the incidence of divorce, which is increasing dramatically in the Arab world with a rate of up to 70%.

The Disadvantages of Poverty and Its Impact on Communities

There are a number of drawbacks that can have a negative impact on many communities, which is due to the widespread poverty and the minimum attention this class is given. It is worth mentioning that this social class represents a large proportion of the whole society, thus leading to a number of shortcomings. Of the most important of these reasons, one can suggest the following:

1. Poverty leads to the breeding of ignorance and the spread of crime, as well as delinquency.
2. Poverty leads to the spread of hostility between the people and lack of security.
3. Poverty leads to fraudulent conduct with others and robbing them of their rights in order to achieve all necessary requirements of life.

These factors can only be found in some poor people as we cannot judge all the poor to be the only perpetrators of crimes and/or that they are ignorant and cunning in pursuit of their goals. Certainly, there seems to a number of people from amongst them who cannot explain their suffering to others or ask for help from anyone as they may feel too inferior or timid to request assistance and continue to suffer in the cycle of poverty.

Unemployment Rates and Its Impact on Communities and Peoples

It is possible to restrict some of the causes of unemployment to two reasons: First, the unwillingness of young people to work, either due to lack of urgency or purpose while searching for work, or the low monthly income that is offered to them. Second, there may be lack of vacancies in keeping with the qualifications of the graduates and job seekers or an unwillingness of the facility to recruit the applying person for reasons only the company is aware of. The rate of unemployment amongst young people in the Arab world has continued to surge upwards. It even involved several university graduates seeking work and whose percentage accounted for 17–25% of the population of the Arab world, as well as unemployment amongst women who make up more than 50% of the population in the Arab world.

Table 2 includes unemployment rates in a number of Arab Gulf states and some Western countries.

Table 2

Country	Unemployment Rates (%)	Gulf States
Saudi Arabia	15	**Reason for Unemployment**
Kuwait	16	1. Reliance on foreign labour.
Bahrain	15	2. Dwindling salaries and long working hours.
United Arab Emirates	5	3. Job dissatisfaction.
Oman	8	4. Administrative corruption and middleman practices.
Egypt	9	Arab Countries
Syria	8	
Yemen	32	**Reason for Unemployment**
Jordan	13	1. Ignorance and low academic performance.
Tunisia	14	
Morocco	9	2. Demographic expansion faced with diminishing job opportunities.
Algeria	16	
Lebanon	14	
Libya	14	3. Administrative corruption and middleman practices.
Sudan	19	

Table 3 includes unemployment rates in some Western countries.

Table 3

Country	Unemployment Rates (%)	Western Countries
United Kingdom	8	**Reason for Unemployment**
United States of America	8	1. Increasing number of graduates from universities and high colleges.
Canada	7	
Netherlands	5	
Germany	7	2. The presence of a social class uninterested in work due to the income support they receive from their respective governments.
Russia	5	
Italy	9	
France	9	

The Impact of Unemployment

Definition of *unemployment*: It is the instance of being out of work for any reason. Most unemployed, in particular poor people, experience a state of void and uneventfulness in their life, leading them to develop negative thoughts in some cases and positive ones on other occasions. Depending on the nature of the person and the environment in which they live, they may develop negative thoughts; thus, those coming from a disadvantageous environment may engage in illegitimate acts such as theft, robbery, vice, and all sorts of deceptive behaviours. On the other hand, if the person lives in a healthy environment, this environment can contribute to his or her development of positive thoughts and taking initiative, such as the completion of his or her studies or choosing alternative routes to working in a public or government job such as taking up a career in agriculture or any business that will help him or her earn a living on a permanent basis.

According to some scientific statistics, unemployment has an impact on mental and physical health, while a large proportion of the unemployed can be so disillusioned that they may experience a sense of failure and inferiority to others. As a result, unemployment can lead to hindered psychological growth, especially with young people who are at the stage of psychological development. This, in turn, may cause a sense of tediousness and monotony, as well as other serious implications, particularly the occurrence of a number of malicious social plights such as theft, fraud, scamming, and vice.

Unemployment can have multiple impacts as far as society is concerned, including people unable to meet the conditions of marriage and increased sexual desires and whims amongst many young people aged between 20 and 30 years. A majority of the unemployed young people who have lost all hopes in a legal relationship through marriage may start searching for alternative solutions, leading to the spread of illicit relationships, temporary marriage, and customary marriage, all of which are not accepted in Muslim Sharia law. Many of these youngsters consider these types of relationships an opportunity to meet their sexual needs, given their inability to meet the costs of legal marriage. The wider implications of these negative impacts lead to a complete lack of sense of responsibility when people decide to end their celibate status.

Without a shred of doubt, being unemployed can reflect negatively and adversely on young people and on society as a whole, with the emergence of some social phenomena that are unfamiliar to the local community, such as drug abuse, theft, rape, and a sense of social injustice. This, in turn, has generated a sense of rebellion, estrangement, and violence, especially in the form of acts of terrorism and rampage. Another type of people may choose to burn inside, which, over time, turns into a sense of frustration, thus creating psychologically devastated youths.

The unemployed can be divided into two types

The first type: People under this category are out of work due to unavailability of job vacancies or as a result of missing out on academic or vocational qualifications that will probably boost the candidates' career chances. With the passing of time, this type amongst the unemployed is the most affected by unemployment.

The second type: It includes those out of work due to their physical inability and also because of their psychological state. People under this category are not actually capable of performing their duties, and in this case, they are entitled to financial help according to their social situation and needs. These financial aids are often estimated between 1,000 and 1,500 SR per month; however, they are undoubtedly unable to meet all their expectations and basic needs. Most of these people are classed as the bottom of the social hierarchy.

- **Causes for Corporate Bankruptcy of Businesses and Organisations**

- **Role of companies and organisations in reducing the scope of the unemployment**

Companies and Institutions

Corporate bankruptcy is one of the problems that can cause serious damage to the owners of the facility and to individuals at the same time. When the company is declared bankrupt, this leads to the laying off all its employees, which can, in turn, affect society as a whole through widespread unemployment. The spread of this social phenomenon is one of the risks that threatens the presence of a secure society due to increased poverty, which, when found in a community, represents a major concern, especially when associated with crime. Sometimes, intentionally, some of those who suffer from the problem of poverty, and in the absence of religious deterrent, resort to inappropriate practices, such as lying, theft, bullying, and inflicting physical harm, which often lead to the crime of murder.

Due to the importance of these firms, it is necessary to develop solutions to help them avoid going bankrupt and re-establish them as viable economic forces that are more secure and well prepared to face future obstacles. There are several reasons for corporate bankruptcy, including financial instability and the inability of firms to meet their financial obligations such as bank loans, as well as the lack of efficient management and human resources in terms of achieving the corporate aims professionally and competently. Added to this is the lack of liquidity and consumer demand for the company's product either due to its high cost price, incompetence, or lack of financial regulation in terms of buying and selling. Other reasons leading owners to declare their firms bankrupt include lack of stability in the financial markets.

According to a financial institution specialised in the monitoring of corporate bankruptcies in the United Kingdom, the number of British companies that have faced financial problems has risen annually since 2009. The latest hazardous warnings issued by the institution analysed Group plc, which monitors corporate bankruptcies, indicate that about 147.863 companies faced financial difficulties during the first three months of 2010, an increase from the year 2009. In an exhaustive report prepared by the company, it stated that the number of companies facing financial difficulties increased by 20% during the last quarter, and it also analysed the very high increase compared to the end of year rise. It noted that the number of companies and institutions going bankrupt will rise to 23,500 in 2011 compared to 21,500 companies in 2010; small companies would be the first affected.

Through the previous report, it can be clearly shown that one of the most leading causes of bankruptcy is the debt overhang. For example, the institution classified approximately 3,018 of the companies with a critical financial situation as those with an estimated debt overhang reaching about 52.8 billion pounds.

Companies declare themselves bankrupt for a number of reasons. The following are the most likely ones:

1. The company's inability to pay off its debts.
2. The inefficiency of the product, lack of consumer demand for it, or failure to provide appropriate service for the various customers.
3. Financial embezzlement.

4. Customer boycott.
5. Losses caused by natural disasters such as that in Japan.
6. Lack of production due to absence of adequate employment.
7. Lack of production due to unavailability of the basic components of the product or scarcity in the market.
8. Inefficient management overseeing the company or negligence by the owner of the firm.
9. Lack of corporate debt rescheduling and failure to repay debts on time, leading to more debts and inability of decision makers to address or control them.

Role of Companies and Organisations in Reducing the Scope of the Unemployment

There is no doubt that there is an active role to play for these businesses and organisations in providing employment opportunities for those interested in work and training them according to the offered activities in order to benefit from the experiences of the trainees and to reduce the size of unemployment as much as possible.

By way of illustration, let us suppose, for example, a company which is specialised in the field of cars. The facility attracts a number of the unemployed who do not hold qualifications to help them obtain jobs and training for a year in the field of car maintenance, while offering a monthly payment according to the company's financial ability. After the provided training of this particular category, the company may offer the participants permanent position according to the training programme provided to them.

The company can also take advantage of applying college graduates and disregard the requirement of experience, as it has the necessary resources to train new employees when required. It is also widely held that an applicant going into a particular job is so keen to understand the details of this professional position within a short time in spite of holding a degree in the same field for which he or she has applied studied and for which he or she has spent a number of years to achieve. Therefore, companies should take into account the number of years studied towards a diploma or bachelor degree as experience gained by the graduate looking for work according to its worth and weight.

All the responsible authorities in the Arab and Western countries should strive to secure employment opportunities for all job seekers as they have a certain number of graduates each year, which would lead to high annual unemployment rates, compared to a rising number of graduates. There are a large number of working people; however, they are still under the poverty line and thus considered as belonging to the unemployment categories for several reasons, with the most important of those being the lack of monthly income and increased costs of living and high prices, making it difficult for low incomers to meet all costs. It should be pointed out that this class of people does not benefit from job stability as they constantly seek to improve their living conditions and enhance their current status, which could, at times, have various negative implications.

A Personal Portfolio (or Personal Account) with Ratios of the Amounts Received

A large number of individuals have so much money; however, they do not know how to use it effectively or are able to manage it appropriately. Some would even find it difficult to account for their expenses in a manner suitable to their basic requirements. Even though they have sufficient income, they still run the risk of falling into eventual financial trouble and being unable to save for a rainy day. Therefore, people who are well off should be more cautious and careful not to overspend on the one hand and be tight with the money on the other. Instead, there is a compromise that may suit all parties, be it employers, traders, or small business owners, to launch a special box, where money is collected according to the method that will be explained in the forthcoming section. This will be used by the person without any external interference, with each person having a personal portfolio, in which an amount is placed on a daily basis with the allocation of 10% of the debited amounts, such as salary, extra income, personal loans, and any additional amounts debited to the account.

The following equation describes the way a personal account works:

Daily amount × 7 = weekly total

The daily amount is an amount placed in the personal portfolio account and is accumulated on a weekly basis (the amount is determined by the owner of the portfolio).

Example: If we have someone who needs to open a personal account, with a daily amount of 15 SAR, the result can be shown as follows:

15 × 7 = 105 SAR – a person can accumulate 105 SAR within a week

Calculating ratios of the received amounts

Amounts received × 10 = percentage allocated to the personal account

Amounts received, of which a proportion is allocated to the personal account include, for example, monthly salaries, extra income, and personal loans.

Example: If the monthly salary is 7000 SAR, a 10% is allocated to one's personal account. The result will be as follows:

7000 × 10/100 = 700 SAR, added to the sum of weeks for a total of:

105 (total of one week) + 700 (10% of the salary) = 805 SAR. This process is repeated for a month, providing the following outcome:

105 (total of one week) × 4 (number of weeks) + 700 (percentage of salary) = 1,120 SAR for the first month.

Table 4 shows the percentage allocated to all incoming amounts.

Table 4: Calculated ratios

Type of Income	Allocated Percentage	Description
Salary	10	Amount earned by employee at the end of each month
Social Security	12	Amount received from the social security service
Bonuses	5	Sums received by some employees such as 'best performance' awards, other than the usual wages
Pensions	10	Sums obtained by retiring employees in the public and government sector
Personal Loans	10	Sums received by people from local and real estate banks, as well as credit and savings companies
Extras	10	Amounts of money obtained by way of cash awards or financial aids
Government spending	5	These are the specified amounts by the government and are allocated in some countries for the unemployed

First: Obtaining the data of the person opening an account and setting up the programme accordingly.

Table 5: The way a personal account works

–	Name of the employee
3500.00 (incoming amount)	Monthly salary
Rent	Type of accommodation
1500.00 (outgoing amount)	Renting charges
89.00 (outgoing amount)	Electric bill
780.00 (outgoing amount)	Vehicle instalments
2369.00 SAR	Net salary
Allocation of ratios	
10%	Salary
10%	Personal loans
10%	Extras

Second: Any of the users whose data is mentioned above can access the programme by using Table 5, in which he or she can input all daily financial information with the allocated percentages of their monthly income.

Third: Selecting a bank account to deposit funds on a weekly or monthly basis, and which is used for this purpose only.

Tables 6 and 7 show this method more clearly according to the data of the employee mentioned above.

Table 6

Days	Date	Amount	Allocated	Total Week	Total	Available	Paid In	The Source	Paid Out
Saturday	29-01-11	34	–	34	34	34			
Sunday	30-01-11	11	–	45	45	45			
Monday	31-01-11	2	350	397	397	397	3.500	Salary	
Tuesday	01-02-11	7	–	404	404	404			
Wednesday	02-02-11	15	–	419	419	419			
Thursday	03-02-11	17	–	436	436	436			
Friday	04-02-11	27	–	463	463	463			
Total						From: 29-01-11 To: 04-02-11			Amount (463.00) SAR

Days	Date	Amount	Allocated	Total Week	Total	Available	Paid In	The Source	Paid Out
Saturday	05-02-11	16	–	16	479	479			
Sunday	06-02-11	29	–	45	508	508			
Monday	07-02-11	19	–	64	527	527			
Tuesday	08-02-11	10	–	74	537	537			
Wednesday	09-02-11	11	–	85	548	548			
Thursday	10-02-11	7	–	92	555	555			
Friday	11-02-11	9	–	101	564	564			
Total						From: 05-02-11 To: 11-02-11			Amount (101.00) SAR

Days	Date	Amount	Allocated	Total Week	Total	Available	Paid In	The Source	Paid Out
Saturday	12-02-11	18	–	18	582	582			
Sunday	13-02-11	9	–	27	591	591			
Monday	14-02-11	10	–	37	601	601			
Tuesday	15-02-11	11	–	48	612	612			
Wednesday	16-02-11	15	–	63	627	627			
Thursday	17-02-11	12	–	75	639	639			
Friday	18-02-11	11	–	86	650	650			
Total						From: 12-02-11 To: 18-02-11			Amount (86.00) SAR

Days	Date	Amount	Allocated	Total Week	Total	Available	Paid In	The Source	Paid Out
Saturday	19-02-11	32	–	32	682	**Withdraw** 682			200
Sunday	20-02-11	8	–	40	690	490			
Monday	21-02-11	9	–	49	699	499			
Tuesday	22-02-11	12	–	61	711	511			
Wednesday	23-02-11	11	–	72	722	522			
Thursday	24-02-11	13	–	85	735	535			
Friday	25-02-11	7	–	92	742	542			
Total						From: 19-01-11 To: 25-02-11			Amount (92.00) SAR

Table 7

Days	Date	Amount	Allocated Percentage	Total Week	Total	Available	Paid In	The Source	Paid Out
Saturday	26-02-11	11		11	753	553			
Sunday	27-02-11	20		31	773	573			
Monday	28-02-11	13		44	786	586			
Tuesday	01-03-11	16	350	410	1.152	Pay 1.152	3.500	Salary	
Wednesday	02-03-11	13		423	1.165	1.165			
Thursday	03-03-11	9		432	1.174	1.174			
Friday	04-03-11	11		443	1.185	1.185			
Total					From: 26-02-11 To: 04-03-11			Amount (443.00) SAR	

Days	Date	Amount	Allocated Percentage	Total Week	Total	Available	Paid In	The Source	Paid Out
Saturday	05-03-11	12		12	1.197	1.197			
Sunday	06-03-11	11		23	1.208	1.208			
Monday	07-03-11	9		32	1.217	1.217			
Tuesday	08-03-11	8		40	1.225	1.225			
Wednesday	09-03-11	14		54	1.239	1.239			
Thursday	10-03-11	22		76	1.261	1.261			
Friday	11-03-11	6		82	1.267	1.267			
Total					From: 05-03-11 To: 11-03-11			Amount (82.00) SAR	

Days	Date	Amount	Allocated Percentage	Total Week	Total	Available	Paid In	The Source	Paid Out
Saturday	12-03-11	10		10	1.277	1.277			
Sunday	13-03-11	8		18	1.285	1.285			
Monday	14-03-11	18		36	1.303	1.303			
Tuesday	15-03-11	12		48	1.315	1.315			
Wednesday	16-03-11	6		54	1.321	1.321			
Thursday	17-03-11	14		68	1.335	1.335			
Friday	18-03-11	9		77	1.344	1.344			
Total					From: 12-03-11 To: 18-03-11			Amount (77.00) SAR	

Days	Date	Amount	Allocated Percentage	Total Week	Total	Available	Paid In	The Source	Paid Out
Saturday	19-03-11	17		17	1.361	1.361			
Sunday	20-03-11	11		28	1.372	1.372			
Monday	21-03-11	26		54	1.398	1.398			
Tuesday	22-03-11	16		70	1.414	1.414			
Wednesday	23-03-11	11		81	1.425	1.425			
Thursday	24-03-11	13		94	1.438	1.438			
Friday	25-03-11	14		108	1.452	1.452			
Total					From: 19-02-11 To: 25-03-11			Amount (108.00) SAR	

Using such model may provide sufficient liquidity for users; hence, pressures and financial crises can be avoided. In case users do not have to draw any amount for a period of 10 months consecutively, users can save up to 38% from their annual income during this period, in case this user has only one source of income. The following table shows how liquidity can be achieved in the event of being used by a number of employees:

Monthly Income	Yearly Income	Percentage of Savings During 10 Months	Saved Amount	
3,500	42,000	38	15,960	SAR
7,800	104,400	38	39,672	
10,400	124,800	38	47,424	

The amounts saved from the annual income can thus play a significant role in avoiding some of the financial pitfalls facing a large number of the population in the thick of the current economic climate

The Most Effective Solution to Combat Poverty, Unemployment, and the Bankruptcy of Companies

There should be a programme to combat bankruptcy and financial bottlenecks, which, in essence, provides a number of loan packages to help reduce corporate bankruptcies and financial bottlenecks for individuals. In addition, the programme raises funds for the poor classes according to their living standards.

Loan packages

A customer needs to deposit a certain amount in order to be able to benefit from the package, which depends on the value of the funds and percentage specified in the packages, along with a number of benefits according to the repayment system and commensurate with all the social classes. There may also be another advantage related to exemption from paying by instalments in case of refinancing within a short period.

Share packages

In this case, the customer purchases the value of the package in order to receive a profit as the rate of profit is not specified.

On the body responsible for the management and operation of the programme

There is a comprehensive study on the project and how it works, as well as on regulations and conditions related to the operation of programme. This study will be shown to the relevant government agency wishing to adopt this project, whose most important objectives are centred on the reduction of corporate bankruptcies and unemployment rates, as well as the provision of liquidity for companies and individuals. The onset of this programme owes so much to the original idea, seeking to help solve many problems of bankruptcy faced by insolvent companies and individuals who suffer from the problem of accumulated debts. This is by allocating 1% for the responsible authority (governmental body) in return for operating the funds of benefiting or participating clients in the programme, as the latter provides customers with loan packages in which they have to deposit a certain amount of money in exchange for financing without incurring any interest, in addition to several other lucrative advantages, including a method of payment that is suitable for the customer and also the advantage of being exempted from instalments in case he or she requests refunding on favourable terms. The programme also provides share packages to suit customers who do not have the ability to commit to pay instalments; as such, they are offered share packages through which they purchase shares in exchange for profits, as the programme is aimed for the more impoverished classes by providing them with this funding option to encourage them to benefit from the programme.

Some of the most important advantages of the programme

The party executing the programme does not have to have capital, provided that it is an investing government body with the potential to invest.

The Price Control Agency and its role in regulating prices

Increasing prices makes it extremely difficult for those who may not be able to cope with this change in the pricing situation. One can also point out the rise in prices in the real estate world, along with a significant increase in spare parts and building materials, which has all taken place as a result of exploitation. When the programme starts running, it should allow a large number of customers access to a wide range of financial facilities and interest-free loans. As a result, some people may take advantage of the situation and thus directly or indirectly contribute to raising prices to such an extent that a customer no longer benefits from this programme and an unavoidable financial crisis ensues. In this case, the price control agency should be set up to regulate prices. While some people argue for a boycott as the answer to this issue, it might similarly be contested that a majority of people see an embargo policy as an inefficient answer, as severe shortages of food, medicines, and some other life necessities that are not indispensable may dissuade them from doing so. Suppose that a certain boycott is to last for one week, it can easily be claimed then that the consumer will be the first victim for not being able to survive without the basic consumer goods that they desperately need.

Will This Programme Play an Effective Role in Poverty Eradication?

Allah's wisdom required that man's life oscillates between happiness and misery, wealth and poverty, and such is the nature of this rapidly changing life that does not wait or last for anyone. How many rich people with all their millions have been forced by the adversities of life to go below the poverty line, and how many poor people's lives have changed dramatically for the better?

Sociologists and other experts confirmed that the world cannot remove the problem of poverty altogether, regardless of the efforts exerted. Even though this phenomenon cannot be totally eradicated, it can still be mitigated.

According to some statistics, they clearly show the percentage of poverty in some countries in the Arab world, with Table 8 giving an approximate percentage of poverty before and after the application of the programme.

Table 8

Countries	Approximate Percentage of Poverty Before the Application of the Programme	Expected Percentage of Poverty After the Application of the Programme	
Egypt	23	5	The reason for this percentage to remain as it is can be ascribed to the fact that a large number of people do not own houses
Yemen	26	6	
Jordon	15	5	
Tones	14	4	
Morocco	14	7	
Algeria	24	5	
Lebanon	10	2	
Mauritania	19	9	
Somalia	45	12	
Sudan	23	11	

Note: The poverty rate specified after the application of the programme includes housing with a large percentage of citizens in some Arab countries not affording to own their own houses, in addition to the impact of the financial crisis on them.

Conclusion

This subject has attracted considerable interest from many segments of the society, regardless of the social class they belong to or the lifestyle they choose to adopt. Therefore, all parties have shown their keenness to achieve as much as they could possibly acquire in order to meet the living costs. In fact, the rising prices have driven people to extremes by demonstrating and burning themselves to death in a clear individual or collective dissatisfaction act against the miserable conditions they live in and to demand their issues to be urgently addressed. Thus, one can conclude that poverty is responsible for all these unfortunate events associated with the poor and the have-nots, who will rise one day against the social injustice imposed on them by their superiors and may cause a serious upheaval and anarchy throughout the country, and worse still, there will be a loss of property and life.

It was crucial to identify and work out answers for a problem experienced by a large number of people. This has been carried out by developing radical solutions to stop this violence, which was caused mainly by poverty and lack of health care. My work has then been focused on offering package programmes for companies and individuals so that they can take advantage of all the benefits provided for them through these packages, namely, loan and share packages, as well as a funding programme for the poor class. The study will propose this programme on the relevant government bodies to be implemented as soon as it is requested by any party willing to adopt it and find out about its details, which can serve the interests of both the responsible party and the customer.

I hope that all government agencies spare some time to study the programme from all angles as it serves the interests of both the responsible party and the client. It should then be applied according to the Islamic Sharia law, which forbids non-Islamic commercial dealings that put off customers and decrease demand for the programme. This programme should also allow a large number of clients to engage in it constructively and take advantage of all the packages it has to offer. This way, there is a better chance to eradicate poverty to a large extent and minimise the problems related to bankruptcy and how it can be reduced.

Blessings and peace upon our Prophet Mohammad and his family

For government bodies and banks only

To request details of the programme and the content of the project, please send a request on behalf of the government agency to the following e-mail:

Threeboxquland-project@live.co.uk
Threeboxquland-general@live.co.uk

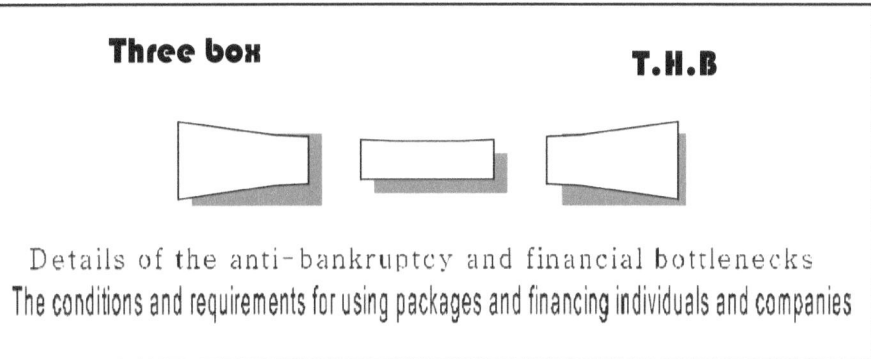

Most references are from the sites on the Internet

Three box

www.quland.org

Prepared by

Mohammed Al Zahrani

Review and coordination

Raid Mohammed Bugis

Translated by

Ali Cherni

Index

The letter *t* following a page number denotes a table.

www.ingramcontent.com/pod-product-compliance
Lightning Source LLC
Chambersburg PA
CBHW021921170526
45157CB00005B/2136